The Bonus Army: The History of the Controversial Protests by American World War I Veterans in 1932

By Charles River Editors

A picture of Bonus Army members scuffling with police

About Charles River Editors

Charles River Editors provides superior editing and original writing services across the digital publishing industry, with the expertise to create digital content for publishers across a vast range of subject matter. In addition to providing original digital content for third party publishers, we also republish civilization's greatest literary works, bringing them to new generations of readers via ebooks.

Sign up here to receive updates about free books as we publish them, and visit Our Kindle Author Page to browse today's free promotions and our most recently published Kindle titles.

Introduction

A picture of Bonus Army protesters camped out at the Capitol

The Bonus Army

"On a day in June, 1932, I saw a dusty automobile truck roll slowly past my house. I saw the unshaven, tired faces of the men who were riding in it standing up. A few were seated at the rear with their legs dangling over the lowered tailboard. On the side of the truck was an expanse of white cloth on which, crudely lettered in black, was a legend, BONUS ARMY." – Evalyn Walsh McLean, *Father Struck it Rich* (1936)

Throughout its history, the United States, like most other countries, has faced the challenge of how to properly reward those have risked, and often given, their lives to defend it. Should they be treated as professionals who were just doing a job? What about those who were drafted, many of whom fought against their own will (or at least preference)? Could anyone really pay them for giving up years of their lives for others? If so, how much was enough to pay a man who had left a comfortable home to live in mud and near starvation? As tough as such questions are in the 21st century age of the professional army, they were that much more complex in the past.

While most people agreed that soldiers should be paid, the question of how much arose and plagued the nation as far back as 1783, two years after the end of the Revolutionary War. In that year, hundreds of men who had fought the British marched into the then capital city of Philadelphia to demand salaries they had been owed for months. Their leader during the war, George Washington, was himself a soldier and wanted to help them but was constrained by a fledgling nation and a Congress that still had much to figure out about governing. At the same time, he was appalled by the mob tactics that were threatening his safety and those of elected officials. He and the members of Congress were retired from the city to nearby Princeton, New Jersey, to consider how to handle the situation. After several weeks of deliberation, they sent the newly organized United States Army back into the city to drive the marchers out.

One of the main questions that fueled the fire of discontent was the issue of military bonuses, that is, extra pay for the difference between what a man earned as a soldier while serving his country and what he might have otherwise earned. This issue remained a bone of contention over the decades that followed and turned up again and again every time the United States went to war. Perhaps because the war lasted such a short time, the veterans of the Spanish-American War, fought over three months in the summer of 1898, did not receive any bonuses. However, this decision came back to haunt the nation decades later when World War I ended. The men who had sailed to Europe to defend American allies from German advances received $60 in the form of bonuses, leading to a public outcry against the government's stinginess. After all, these men were not even defending their own families and loved ones from attack but were protecting foreign governments. Why, many wondered, should their loved ones suffer from the wages lost on European shores?

The unrest culminated in one of the most controversial protests of the 20th century, that organized by the Bonus Army in Washington, D.C. in the spring and summer of 1932. The Bonus Army consisted mostly of World War I veterans who were seeking to redeem bonus certificates from the World War Adjusted Compensation Act of 1924, which had stipulated that they could not be redeemed until 1945. Unfortunately, the economic plight had left so many of them struggling that they were seeking the vitally necessary money right away.

Tens of thousands of World War I veterans came to the capital with virtually nothing and erected makeshift camps, all but waiting for a reward. Eventually, what they got was violence, meted out by one of America's most famous generals: Army Chief of Staff Douglas MacArthur. After the Bonus Army began camping out in Washington D.C., ironically using supplies that MacArthur himself had issued to them, Washington grew impatient with their demands and politicians started calling for their forced expulsion. When police confronted the Bonus Army, shots were fired and several veterans were killed.

After that, Hoover ordered MacArthur to use the military. Certainly he imagined the "Bonus Army" as some kind of communist front, and certainly he came close to exceeding President Hoover's orders. Fortunately however, casualties were light, with one fatality, in contrast to the half dozen killed the day before by the police. Nevertheless, the sight of soldiers marching on old veterans and inflicting violence upon them was a public relations fiasco, and MacArthur has long been criticized for the actions. In fact, MacArthur was so sensitive to the criticism that he later sued journalists who called his actions "unwarranted, unnecessary, insubordinate, harsh and brutal" for defamation.

The Bonus Army: The History of the Controversial Protests by American World War I Veterans in 1932 chronicles the notorious protests and the violence that ensued. Along with pictures of important people, places, and events, you will learn about the Bonus Army like never before, in no time at all.

The Bonus Army: The History of the Controversial Protests by American World War I Veterans in 1932

Chapter 1: Its Failure to Feed And Care For Them

"Aside from its failure to feed and care for them, aside from their illegal and inhuman exilement by the Army, and over and above all these considerations, was the fact that President Hoover then laid down a hard and ignoble policy to guide his course of action throughout the 'Great Depression' which policy wrought his political defeat, wrought the collapse of the Republican Party, and prolonged the depression. I refer, of course, to his declared policy that the Federal Government could not appropriate and expend money to aid the poor and hungry citizens who might otherwise freeze, hunger and perish. Such financial responsibility, he declared, was the sole duty of the States, the counties, cities, towns and charity. Doggedly he stuck to this principle. Stubbornly he applied it to all. Rigidly he applied it to the 'Bonus Marchers' stranded in Washington. That now famous pilgrimage to the Capital, with all its alarm and tragedy, so dramatized the President's harsh economic policy that it was repudiated by the people. So stubborn was President Hoover in adhering to his declared policy of 'no-Federal-aid-for-the poor' that he had it incorporated into the Republican Party platform (1932) soon thereafter. From that day he seemed doomed to defeat for reelection, and his Party doomed to fall. It proved to be the death knell of the 'Old Deal' and the forerunner of the 'New.'" – John Henry Bartlett, *The Bonus March and the New Deal* (1937)

The beginning of the 20th century was in many ways a high water mark for American patriotism, and the fervor lasted well past the end of World War I. In September 1920, James H. Trewin of Cedar Rapids, Iowa, addressed a large audience of veterans gathered there for the Second Annual Convention of the American Legion to discuss, among other things, a bill demanding bonuses for veterans: "It may seem to you—It seems so to me sometimes—that the American people have forgotten your sacrifices and the victories you won. But that is not the case. In the hearts of the people you will find the love and homage they hold for you and the people, I am sure, want to do Justice to the members of the Legion. It is your privilege and your duty to get it. I'm not one of those who will quibble as to what justice is. Knowing you as I do I am willing to leave it to you to say to the American people what shall be Justice to those who have been killed, those who have been wounded and those who have been deprived of what they had. You will find me for one raising my voice in support of your action. I read the other day that there are about 75,000 of your comrades mentally afflicted because of their experiences in the war, and that the government had lost track of them. During the war we who remained home learned the lessons of service and the spirit of service. Shall we forget the lessons of service and the spirit of service while you are among us? I say no. There should be an organization in every community to reach out a helping hand to those in distress, especially the former service men. You men adapted a preamble to your constitution, which I have seen in print but not in newspapers as much as it ought to be."

Cinderella stamp issued in support of the Bonus Army by Steve Strummer

James H. Trewin

Based on protests and riots that he had seen break out in the past, Colonel Matthew Tinley urged the men gathered together that day to take care in their actions, lest they bring disrepute on themselves and their cause. At the same time, he insisted, "Legislation is going to be needed. Pitiful indeed is it that men who have served their country at such great cost have to lower themselves for that which is justly theirs. An organized effort must be put forth to see that the service man has justice done him by national and state governments. We are not asking for anything that is improper. The only improper thing is the name of 'bonus'. A bonus is something over and above a fully compensated service. I don't care how long a man served. The intentions of all were identical. The affairs of private life were put behind them. If any person or persons say the pittance of $30 a month was compensation in full and a small additional amount estimated on the number of months in service is a bonus they are mistaken."

Thanks to the words of the Legion and other veterans' groups, Congress passed the World War Adjusted Compensation Act, also known as the Bonus Act, on May 19, 1924. According to a statement prepared by Senator Selden Spencer a few weeks earlier, the bill "applies to practically every veteran in military and naval forces in the United States between April 5, 1917, and November 12, 1918," and "provides for the payment of $1.25 for each day of oversea service and $1 a day for each day of home service (excluding the first 60 days of service, which was taken care of by the original bonus of $60), with a limit of $625 for oversea service and $500 for home service. It does not apply to anyone with a grade above that of captain in the Army and its relative rank in the other branches of service."

Spencer

The bill also contained four plans for the soldier's use:

"a. For adjusted service pay, provided that if the amount coming to the ex-service man is $50 or less, it is payable at once.

b. To receive vocational training aid.

c. To receive farm or home aid.

d. To receive land settlement aid."

The provision that later proved to be the most controversial was the one concerning the "adjusted service certificate." According to the synopsis, "If the ex-service man elects to take an adjusted service certificate, he receives a certificate for the amount due him…and…for an amount equal to 25 per cent of the actual service compensation, and in to this, interest on the full amount at the rate of 4 ½ per cent compounded annually for 20 years, so that the actual face value of the adjusted service certificate which the ex-service man had is about three times the amount due him…. This certificate is payable in 20 years; that is, on or before September 20, 1942. If the holder should die before his maturity, then the full amount is immediately payable to the person designated by him as his beneficiary, or, failing such designation, to his estate." Each veteran who had fought received his certificate on his birthday in 1925, so they were not actually redeemable until 1945 unless he died.

In passing the Compensation Bill, Congress also authorized the veterans to borrow up to 22.5% of their certificates' value before it was matured. The assumption was that the men would use this money to buy small businesses or purchase homes, thus stoking the American economy. However, some of them borrowed the money to invest in the burgeoning stock market, only to lose it in the great crash of 1929. Now they not only had no money to pay back the loan, they also, in many cases, had no jobs to earn any more. Under pressure from the men to have more access to what they believed was rightfully theirs, Congress voted in 1931 to increase the amount that could be borrowed to 50% of each certificate's value. Many men used this to borrow the funds they needed to feed and shelter their families, but this money was soon gone and the men returned to Congress to plead to be allowed to cash in their certificates for their full value.

President Herbert Hoover opposed this move because he was afraid that the sudden draw from the Federal coffers of billions of dollars would force him to raise taxes on an already suffering populace. He wrote to Senator Reed Smoot on February 18, 1931, "I have supported, and the nation should maintain, the important principle that when men have been called into jeopardy of their very lives in protection of the Nation, then the Nation as a whole incurs a special obligation beyond that to any other groups of its citizens. These obligations cannot be wholly met with dollars and cents. But good faith and gratitude require that protection be given to them when in ill health, distress and in need. Over 700,000 World War Veterans or their dependents are today receiving monthly allowances for these reasons. The country should not be called upon, however, either directly or indirectly, to support or make loans to those who can by their own efforts support themselves. By far the largest part of the huge sum proposed in this bill is to be available to those who are not in distress. The acute depression and unemployment create a situation of unusual economic sensitiveness, much more easily disturbed at this time than in normal times by the consequences of this legislation, and such action may quite well result in a prolongation of this period of unemployment and suffering in which veterans will themselves suffer with others."

President Hoover

Reed Smoot

Having said that, Hoover went on to put forward his concerns about the effect that paying out so many bonuses would have on the American economy: "By our expansion of public construction for assistance to unemployment and other relief measures, we have imposed upon ourselves a deficit in this fiscal year of upwards of $500,000,000 which must be obtained by issue of securities to the investing public. This bill may possibly require the securing of a further billion of money likewise from the public. Beyond this, the Government is faced with a billion dollars of early maturities of outstanding debts which must be refunded aside from constant renewals of a very large amount of temporary Treasury obligations. The additional burdens of this project cannot but have damaging effect at a time when all effort should be for the rehabilitation of employment through resumption of commerce and industry. There seems to be a misunderstanding in the proposal that the Government securities already lodged with the

Treasury to the amount of over $700,000,000 as reserve against these certificates constitute available cash to meet this potential liability. The cash required by the veterans can only be secured by the sale of these securities to the public. The legislation is defective in that this $700,000,000 of Government securities is wholly inadequate to mend either a potential liability of $1,280,000,000 or approximately $1,000,000,000 estimated as possible by the Administrator of Veterans' Affairs, and provision would need to be made at once for this deficiency."

Finally, Hoover dealt with what was perhaps the most pressing and emotionally tangible argument for the bill, concluding, "The one appealing argument for this legislation is for veterans in distress. The welfare of the veterans as a class is inseparable from that of the country. Placing a strain on the savings needed for rehabilitation of employment by a measure which calls upon the Government for a vast sum beyond the call of distress, and so adversely affecting our general situation, will in my view not only nullify the benefits to the veteran but inflict injury to the country as a whole."

All the while, the Veterans of Foreign Wars and other such organizations continued to press for the payout. In April 1931, Commander-in-Chief Paul C. Wolman observed, "Between two and three billions of dollars will be placed in circulation if Congress sees fit to act on this suggestion. Loans floated by the government for this purpose will provide money that will stimulate virtually every channel of business endeavor. The bulk of this money will undoubtedly be spent for the payment of debts already incurred by veterans in distress, while the more fortunate ex-service men can make good use of this money to feed and clothe their families, for the building of homes and for the purchase of little necessities and luxuries that have thus far been denied. Instead of making the ex-service man, who needs this money, hold these promissory notes issued by Uncle Sam, why not transfer these certificates to the lands of capitalists who can best afford waiting until 1945 before these notes mature. … The manner in which thousands of veterans demonstrated their need for funds by borrowing the value of these certificates as the loan value automatically increased on January 1, is ample evidence of the emergency that exists among those who served during the World war. When congress passed the World war adjusted compensation act in 1924 it officially acknowledged this country's debt to those who served in the war with Germany. The debt is a just one, and deserving of recognition now at a time when these funds would contribute so materially to the welfare of the ex-service men and the nation at large."

In his contemporary book about the Bonus Army, *The Bonus March and the New Deal* (1937), John Henry Bartlett summed up the feelings of the veterans at the beginning of the Great Depression: "Begging in vain for a job from one end of the country to the other, at a time when millions were doing the same, he had come here, at last, from a bread line in Chicago, and he and Buddy Carlson had trekked from among Oakland's unemployed sufferers to the home city of their fatherland, flags in hand, seeking that 'compensation' which they felt might now be paid them, or praying for labor that they might no longer live as paupers and tramps. But, alas, this 'compensation' had been denied them, labor had been denied them, and the crude shacks in which they slept at night were now being denied them. … The death-dealing missiles also bequeathed to their legal representatives the right by law to receive the bonus money, at once, which would have saved their lives had it been paid before. … But it was poverty that killed you."

Chapter 2: This Sum Was Not Nearly Enough

"Did not Congress vote $100,000 to pay the fares home of the Bonus Marchers, may be asked. To this I answer 'Yes and no.' The vote was not to 'give' the expense money to them, but to make a 'loan' to be deducted from what the Government owes them, in 1945, with interest. But even this sum was not nearly enough to send them all anywhere. They had been kicked underfoot by the depression too long to have homes. Many were ejected for nonpayment of rent. There were thousands of unemployed at their original home towns, else they would never have left. They wanted work more than the bonus. Some whole counties and towns in coal-mining districts, for instance, had all their inhabitants idle. This was true particularly in Pennsylvania, West Virginia and Kentucky. … Those who would not accept this loan to go home had another good reason. It was spending money without benefit, as they would have nothing when they got somewhere else. … Should not an overseas veteran when absolutely destitute be made to feel at home in Washington? … It was just too bad to disillusion him. That was the attitude of those who had no place to go." – John Henry Bartlett, *The Bonus March and the New Deal* (1937)

With no jobs and often no homes, a number of men decided to go to Washington in person to plead with Congress for the money owed them. In January 1932, 25,000 veterans marched from Pennsylvania to Washington, D.C. They were led by Father James Renshaw Cox, a Roman Catholic priest who was active in politics and the labor movement. According to an *Associated Press* article published on January 7, "The leader of ten thousand unemployed men was received in friendly fashion by President Hoover today but was given no assurance that his request for work and help would be met. Father James R. Cox of Pittsburgh, after giving congress and the president a petition for aid said the president had told him everything that the government could do was being done and that there was no chance of doing things suddenly outside of the regular channels. 'I told the president,' Father Cox said, 'that unless immediate relief is given, God help the country.' He went to the White House after an orderly demonstration on Capitol Hill at which he had given the petition to Senator Davis and Representative Kelly of Pennsylvania. It later was read in the house. … Father Cox said a count by police disclosed 2,248 cars and trucks already here and a steady stream of stragglers still coming In. He estimated there were than 20,000 in the group. The priest spent most of the night going from billet to billet talking with his men and urging them to keep up their spirits. While they waited to begin the march some of the men began singIng to the accompaniment of guitars and harmonicas. A band from the North Braddock, Pennsylvania, firs department, headed the march."

Cox

   As for the men he was leading, they were mostly hungry and cold, not belligerent. In fact, the Bonus March began as one of the most peaceful, inoffensive gatherings of citizens ever held in the nation's capital. The article continued, "Stiff from a night spent in crumped and crowded sleeping quarters, many of them under blankets drenched by the rainstorm that ushered them into the city, the followers of Father James R. Cox of Pittsburgh consumed hundreds of gallons of steaming coffee and thousands of doughnuts and rolls. Eight army rolling kitchens from Fort Myer provided the food. Informed that breakfast would be served, thousands of the marchers, most of whom had had nothing to eat since noon yesterday, descended on the kitchens in droves. The feeding started at 7:30 and continued for three hours but the supply of rolls and doughnuts furnished by District of Columbia relief organizations ran out before everyone was served."

One of the biggest but likely unfounded concerns on the part of the government was that this group of patriotic soldiers was somehow part of a Communist front seeking to bring down the American government in the same way the Russian monarchy had fallen about 15 years earlier. However, the men themselves wanted it made clear that they were loyal to their country and meant no trouble. The reporter writing the above article observed, "Their journey was in vivid contrast to that body of demonstrators that concentrated here at the beginning of congress to chant 'The Internationale' in the streets of the capital. Extra police…were there more as traffic directors than in anticipation trouble. The riot guns and tear gas bombs with which they were armed for the December demonstrators were absent. … More than 100 extra policemen were drawn up in front of the capitol but such jobless men as came were admitted freely although some of the doors were kept locked to permit a careful police scrutiny of those entering the main portals. There was no sign of disorder. The visitors inspected with the apparent interest of a group of tourist sightseers, their subdued manner contrasting sharply with the shouted demands of the marchers led by Communist sympathizers a month ago. Clad In lumberjack coats and sweaters, many wandered through the corridors of the capitol under the resplendent chandeliers. The great majority had been fed and were in a pleasant mood. 'We ain't Communists, and we ain't looking for trouble,' one of them loudly proclaimed, as George U Ewing, a Pittsburgh grocery man, one of the leaders, arrived."

The march concluded at Arlington National Cemetery, where Cox told his followers, "You will live to tell your grandchildren of this event, of the courteous treatment you have been accorded by everyone in the city. This is God's country and under God we are going to keep it that way. Today you have asked only for your God-given right to work. So long as I live and have a tongue and can breathe, I will work for you and all the common people." That said, Cox concluded with an ominous tone: "If our efforts do not succeed, we are ready for anything, even bloodshed."

Such was the respectability with which the 25,000 marchers conducted themselves that Gifford Pinchot, the Republican governor of Pennsylvania, supported their claims. Of course, it is only fair to note that Pinchot was planning a run against Hoover for the Republican presidential nomination and no doubt hoped to persuade Cox's followers to back him. At the same time, Cox was seen by many in the Church as a hero, with the *Pittsburgh Catholic* writing on January 14, "The pilgrimage …if it does nothing else, brought to the nation's attention the fact that Catholic priests are vitally interested in the social and economic welfare of the people of all faiths, and that the downtrodden and oppressed will continue to find as they have always found, a true friend and champion in the parish priest."

Pinchot

At the time, however, many in America saw Catholic priests as only slightly less dangerous than Communists. Hoover had Cox investigated and learned much to his fury that his own Secretary of the Treasury, Andrew Mellon, had backed the marchers, including ordering his Gulf Oil gas stations to provide those driving to Washington for the march with free fuel to make sure they made it to their destination. Mellon soon resigned his post.

Mellon

Chapter 3: Poor Folks Are Allowed to Starve

"A well-informed humanitarian suggested that these men be sworn in as a sort of auxiliary to the Army and allowed to remain in the barracks for a while. This would give the Army a legal right to feed them. Some hoped for this. President Hoover said 'No.' It is error to say that the Government is so poor it must neglect its old soldiers. Our Government is not poor. It is not near broke. Federal credit is excellent. It should be drawn on. The Federal Government must give before poor folks are allowed to starve. There must be provided one of two alternatives, work or dole, before suffering is permitted. We cannot dodge that conclusion. And the Federal Government must give, not simply loan as a banker at a profit. It must give at once to stop rioting and revolution." – John Henry Bartlett, *The Bonus March and the New Deal* (1937)

When the marchers in Cox's Army returned home in January 1932, many believed that they had made a significant difference in the course of history and that the American government had heard their pleas and would act on them. However, while there were those in Congress who backed the veterans' requests, Hoover continued to oppose any sort of payouts, stating publicly in March 1932, "Informal polls of the House of Representatives have created apprehension in the country that a further bonus bill of $2 billion or thereabouts for World War veterans will be passed. I wish to state again that I am absolutely opposed to any such legislation. I made this position clear at the meeting of the American Legion in Detroit last September 21, and the Legion has consistently supported that position. I do not believe any such legislation can become law. Such action would undo every effort that is being made to reduce Government expenditures and balance the budget. The first duty of every citizen of the United States is to build up and sustain the credit of the United States Government. Such an action would irretrievably undermine it."

Thus, not long after Cox's Army went home, another group began to plan their own march into Washington. In late May 1932, thousands of World War I veterans descended on Washington D.C. from around the country, demanding that Congress give them the military bonuses they had been promised. John Dos Passos, writing for *The New Republic* in June of that year, mentioned one such group: "A bunch of out-of-work ex-service men in Portland, Oregon, figured they needed their bonus now; 1945 would be too late, only buy wreaths for their tombstones. They figured out, too, that the bonus paid now would tend to liven up business, particularly the retail business in small towns; might be just enough to tide them over till things picked up. So three hundred of them started east in old cars and trucks, hitchhiking, riding on freight trains. By the time they reached Council Buffs (Iowa) they found other groups all over the country were rebelling against their veterans' organizations and getting the same idea. It was an Army. They organized it as such and nicknamed it the Bonus Expedition Force."

At first, those making their way across the country were greeted with skepticism and even fear. The war years had emphasized to the American people the importance of pulling together and supporting the government's initiatives. Now these men were seen by many as malcontents trying to undermine American life in a time of crisis. In his 1934 book *The Dream of Golden Mountains*, Malcom Cowley recalled, "A few weeks later there was more talk of revolution when the Bonus Expeditionary Force descended on Washington. The BEF was a tattered army consisting of veterans from every state in the Union; most of them were old-stock Americans from smaller industrial cities where relief had broken down. All unemployed in 1932, all living on the edge of hunger, they remembered that the government had made them a promise for the future. It was embodied in a law that Congress had passed some years before, providing "adjusted compensation certificates" for those who had served in the Great War; the certificates were to be redeemed in dollars, but not until 1945. Now the veterans were hitchhiking and stealing rides on freight cars to Washington, for the sole purpose, they declared, of petitioning Congress for immediate payment of the soldiers' bonus. They arrived by hundreds or thousands every day in June. Ten thousand were camped on marshy ground across the Anacostia River, and ten thousand others occupied a number of half-demolished buildings between the Capitol and the White House. They organized themselves by states and companies and chose a commander named Walter W. Waters, an ex-sergeant from Portland. Oregon, who promptly acquired an aide-de-camp and a pair of highly polished leather puttees. Meanwhile the veterans were listening to speakers of all political complexions, as the Russian soldiers had done in 1917. Many radicals and some conservatives thought that the Bonus Army was creating a revolutionary situation of an almost classical type."

Evalyn Walsh McLean, a Washington socialite whose husband owned the *Washington Post*, also wrote about their arrival. "On a day in June, 1932, I saw a dusty automobile truck roll slowly past my house. I saw the unshaven, tired faces of the men who were riding in it standing up. A few were seated at the rear with their legs dangling over the lowered tailboard. On the side of the truck was an expanse of white cloth on which, crudely lettered in black, was a legend, BONUS ARMY. Other trucks followed in a straggling succession, and on the sidewalks of Massachusetts Avenue where stroll most of the diplomats and the other fashionables of Washington were some ragged hikers, wearing scraps of old uniforms. The sticks with which they strode along seemed less canes than cudgels. They were not a friendly-looking lot, and I learned they were hiking and riding into the capital along each of its radial avenues; that they had come from every part of the continent. It was not lost on me that those men, passing anyone of my big houses, would see in such rich shelters a kind of challenge. I was burning, because I felt that crowd of men, women, and children never should have been permitted to swarm across the continent. But I could remember when those same men, with others, had been cheered as they marched down Pennsylvania Avenue. While I recalled those wartime parades, I was reading in the newspapers that the bonus army men were going hungry in Washington."

McLean

McLean soon had reason to change her opinion of the marchers and their presence in the capital. "That night I woke up before I had been asleep an hour. I got to thinking about those poor devils marching around the capital. Then I decided that it should be a part of my son Jock's education to see and try to comprehend that marching. It was one o'clock, and the Capitol was beautifully lighted. I wished then for the power to turn off the lights and use the money thereby saved to feed the hungry. When Jock and I rode among the bivouacked men I was horrified to see plain evidence of hunger in their faces; I heard them trying to cadge cigarettes from one another. Some were lying on the sidewalks, unkempt heads pillowed on their arms. A few clusters were shuffling around. I went up to one of them, a fellow with eyes deeply sunken in his head. 'Have you eaten?' He shook his head. Just then I saw General Glassford, superintendent of the Washington police. He said, 'I'm going to get some coffee for them.' 'All right,' I said, 'I am going to Childs'.'"

Pelham Davis Glassford

What McLean did next was an example, perhaps, of all that was good in 1930s America, as she reached past her own preconceived notions about what groups of people were up to in order meet the needs of individuals.

"It was two o'clock when I walked into that white restaurant. A man came up to take my order. 'Do you serve sandwiches? I want a thousand,' I said. 'And a thousand packages of cigarettes.'

'But, lady - '

'I want them right away. I haven't got a nickel with me, but you can trust me. I am Mrs. McLean.'

Well, he called the manager into the conference, and before long they were slicing bread with a machine; and what with Glassford's coffee also (he was spending his own money) we two fed all the hungry ones who were in sight."

The men and their families soon set up camps in the swampy marsh of the District of Columbia's Anacostia Flats. John Henry Bartlett regularly visited the camps and wrote in his book on the Bonus Army, "My observation, which during the eight weeks was very extensive, is that it would be difficult to pick out 10,000 extremely poverty ridden folks who were as loyal to their country as these men. Some of us felt they were almost obsessed with loyalty. They insisted on having a flag on every hut. If any group of them had any place to go together they would invariably carry the colors, and they did have a few rather large flags. They used to say, 'The flag that we defended will defend us.' I did not talk with any one of them who had in his heart any desire to overturn the Government by force. They did seem to feel that the money bag of the Government was in control of a few people who refused to let go even when men were starving, and they had a crusade spirit that the Government should be returned to the people. I went to some of their religious meetings, held in a big tent, and I always observed a spirit of patient forbearance, and humble trust in God. Their speakers would say by way of encouragement that there were others who were worse off than they, and then would read from the book of Job. I visited the Salvation Army tent quite frequently. There were hundreds of books and magazines which had been given them. They had several extemporized benches or tables, and the tent was always full of men writing letters, and they were more appreciative of a postage stamp than of a cigarette."

A makeshift camp erected by members of the Bonus Army

Bartlett was also impressed by the orderliness with which the camp was run. The men worked hard to make sure that their makeshift neighborhood, constructed largely from found materials, was a safe, orderly place, policing it themselves to keep things quiet and respectable. Anyone wanting to move into the camp had to show proof of his honorable discharge from the United States military. Bartlett wrote, "They had a little Post Office. I think the mail came to the Chief of Police. He sent it to the Salvation Army tent, and there they had secured some pigeonhole boxes and put up a sign "B. E. F. Post Office." I never saw any fighting among them. They had a few of their own men with puny short sticks going about the camp as Policemen, and Chief Glassford also had a few of his regular policemen around. The veterans' police and the regular city police were friendly and worked together. I saw no signs of liquor except once, and what called my attention to that was that two or three of the bonus policemen had a man who was partly intoxicated and were forcibly ejecting him from the Camp. I heard one of them say as they were doing it, 'You are not coming in here to give us a bad name.' I assumed that he was not a bonus man. A few Communists who were present there, as they are everywhere, would occasionally scatter some Communist literature by night. This the bonus men would report, pick up, and destroy as soon as possible. They chucked Communists out of their Camps as fast as they could find one, until finally the camps were comparatively free from Communists and agitators, those under Pace being billeted in one of the small groups in the down town area by themselves. Some right wing boys once took one group of 100 Communists, made them renounce Communism and take the loyal oath of the B. E. F. [Bonus Expeditionary Force]"

Chapter 4: I Have No Home

"It is true that these veterans were fearing two things quite constantly. They were fearing that food supply, which never was over a day ahead and sometimes a day behind, would entirely give out. I have heard Commander Waters address them saying that he believed he could keep them from starving. He said, 'If you have to go one day, just tighten up your belts and stand it. I don't think the American people will let us starve. I will do the best I can for you.' The other fear that they had was that the rumors were true which said they would be driven off by the Government. They scarcely believed this, and yet they did fear it. They were very friendly to Glassford, always gave him a cheer when he came, but they had some intimation that his patient policy might be intercepted. This fear became a fact. I talked with an intelligent fellow from Flint, Michigan, who said to me: 'There is no use of my going back there. The automobile factories are all shut down and many thousands are tramping the streets. If I don't starve I am better off here. I have no home.' I talked with another fellow and asked him how he happened to come to Washington. He fished out of a deep breeches pocket a paper, unfolded it and showed it to me -- a bonus certificate. He said, 'I saw on here that Washington was where Uncle Sam held out and where the money would be. I had been knocking around through various States and was then in Florida, so I started hitch-hiking for Washington, and here I am.'" – John Henry Bartlett, *The*

Bonus March and the New Deal (1937)

On June 15, the House of Representatives passed the Wright Patman Bonus Bill, which promised to move up the date that the veterans could claim their promised bonuses. However, upon hearing that the Senate would likely defeat the bill, the Bonus Army marched from the camp to the steps of the Capitol on June 17. Not surprisingly, many were concerned that there might be trouble with so many present in such a small space, but it turned out they had little to worry about. According to an *Associated Press* report, "The voice of Representative [Thomas] Blanton, (D.. Texas) urging the veterans to remember that 'your friends are counting on your good conduct,' was almost drowned out by cheers from the bonus army. Blanton told the veterans that if they are patient 'the bonus matter will be settled to your satisfaction.' 'I don't think there is a man here who wouldn't rather have a job than cash payment of the bonus," Brookhart told the Senate. As the Iowan proceeded with his address the veterans in the galleries leaned forward intently. They maintained perfect order. On the floor, the customary noises were absent, members—regardless of their views on the question—paid close attention."

Blanton

In speaking on behalf of the bill, Senator Smith W. Brookhart said, "The bonus army might as well assemble here as anywhere. They have no jobs. I can see no reason why 100,000, 200,000 or 500,000 shouldn't assemble here. The government of the United States had done much for everybody but the common people. This bill will raise commodity prices and will help agriculture. The bonus bill is not only in the interest of the soldiers themselves but the great agricultural interests, the seven or eight million unemployed and it is sound business. It is the only patriotic course this country can take under the flag these men followed."

Brookhart

In spite of Brookhart's stirring words, the Senate defeated the bill soundly by a vote of 62 to 18. With that, many thought that the marchers would now return to their homes. McLean, who had continued to reach out to those staying in the city and even took some into her own home, recalled:

"One day Waters, the so-called commander, came to my house and said: 'I'm desperate. Unless these men are fed, I can't say what won't happen to this town.' With him was his wife, a little ninety-three-pounder, dressed as a man, her legs and feet in shiny boots. Her yellow hair was freshly marceled.

'She's been on the road for days,' said Waters, 'and has just arrived by bus.'

I thought a bath would be a welcome change; so I took her upstairs to that guest bedroom my father had designed for King Leopold. I sent for my maid to draw a bath, and told the young woman to lie down.

'You get undressed,' I said, 'and while you sleep I'll have all your things cleaned and pressed.'

'Oh, no,' she said, 'not me. I'm not giving these clothes up. I might never see them again.'

"Her lip was out, and so I did not argue. She threw herself down on the bed, boots and all, and I tiptoed out.

"That night I telephoned to Vice-President Charlie Curtis. I told him I was speaking for Waters, who was standing by my chair. I said: 'These men are in a desperate situation, and unless something is done for them, unless they are fed, there is bound to be a lot of trouble. They have no money, nor any food.' Charlie Curtis told me that he was calling a secret meeting of senators and would send a delegation of them to the House to urge immediate action on the Howell bill, providing money to send the bonus army members back to their homes."

The problem, of course, was that most of the members of the Bonus Army did not want to leave. Each had his own reasons, but in general, most felt that they had little or nothing to go back to, and that at least in Washington they had made friends and established relationships with people who understood their problems and concerns. The families were getting regular support from veterans organizations from around the country, and it somehow seemed more respectable to stay and fight for their rights than to run home and go on the dole. As a result, thousands stayed as the city became hotter, both literally and figuratively, with the onset of summer.

Chapter 5: Their Final, Swift Evacuation

"This is a narrative concerning the pilgrimage of 10,000 'Bonus Marchers,' their spontaneous hitch-hiking from all angles of the United States to the Capital, their eight weeks of patient waiting and painful camping in the open, or in extemporized shelters, their daily search for food, and their final swift evacuation from Washington by police; by cavalry, infantry, tanks and machine guns from the United States Army, commanded by General MacArthur, hastily called out by the then Secretary of War, Hurley, on a peremptory command from President Herbert Hoover, the Commander-in-Chief, July 28th,1932. This nighttime exilement, to desolate country roads, of old soldiers, and their families; of unarmed, unfed, unresisting World War veterans, by means of gas, fire, bayonet and gun, came to have momentous significance in American history, not only because two veterans and a child were killed, many veterans and their wives gassed and wounded, and all needlessly humiliated, but because, through its amazing influence, a great Federal question became agitated, brought to the fore, and settled right. ... So, by that ex parte battle, we may have been saved from a threatened insurrection. By it the eyes of America were well opened. The suffering of the Bonus Marchers contributed to bring about a better day for all the poor." – John Henry Bartlett, *The Bonus March and the New Deal* (1937)

By the end of July, Hoover had had enough of men he considered enemies of peace and order camping near the White House and Capitol. Then, early in the morning on July 28, he received the following letter: "The Commissioners of the District of Columbia regret to inform you that during the past few hours, circumstances of a serious character have arisen in the District of Columbia which have been the cause of unlawful acts of large numbers of so-called 'bonus marchers', who have been in Washington for some time past. This morning, officials of the Treasury Department, seeking to clear certain areas within the Government triangle in which there were numbers of these bonus marchers, met with resistance. They called upon the Metropolitan Police Force for assistance and a serious riot occurred. Several members of the Metropolitan Police were injured, one reported seriously. The total number of bonus marchers greatly outnumbered the police; the situation is made more difficult by the fact that this area contains thousands of brickbats and these were used by the rioters in their attack upon the police. In view of the above, it is the opinion of the Major and Superintendent of Police, in which the Commissioners concur, that it will be impossible for the Police Department to maintain law and order except by the free use of firearms which will make the situation a dangerous one; it is believed, however, that the presence of Federal troops in some number will obviate the seriousness of the situation and result in far less violence and bloodshed."

This proved to be just the opportunity that he was waiting for. Later that same morning, he announced, "For some days police authorities and Treasury officials have been endeavoring to persuade the so-called bonus marchers to evacuate certain buildings which they were occupying without permission. These buildings are on sites where Government construction is in progress and their demolition was necessary in order to extend employment in the District and to carry forward the Government's construction program. This morning the occupants of these buildings were notified to evacuate and at the request of the police did evacuate the buildings concerned. Thereafter, however, several thousand men from different camps marched in and attacked the police with brickbats and otherwise injuring several policemen, one probably fatally."

What Hoover failed to mention was that his own Attorney General, William D. Mitchell, had ordered the police to remove the men. He also said nothing about the fact that the police killed two veterans, William Hushka and Eric Carlson, during the scuffle.

William Mitchell.

Regardless, the violence provided Hoover with the excuse he needed to order the veterans removed once and for all. He stated, "I have received the attached letter from the Commissioners of the District of Columbia stating that they can no longer preserve law and order in the District. In order to put an end to this rioting and defiance of civil authority, I have asked the Army to assist the District authorities to restore order. Congress made provision for the return home of the so-called bonus marchers who have for many weeks been given every opportunity of free assembly, free speech, and free petition to the Congress. Some 5,000 took advantage of this arrangement and have returned to their homes."

Warming to his topic, Hoover insisted that those remaining within the city did so out of either malice or ignorance: "An examination of a large number of names discloses the fact that a considerable part of those remaining are not veterans; many are communists and persons with criminal records. The veterans amongst these numbers are no doubt unaware of the character of their companions and are being led into violence which no government can tolerate. I have asked the Attorney General to investigate the whole incident and to cooperate with the District civil authorities in such measures against leaders and rioters as may be necessary."

By the time Hoover finished speaking, Patrick Hurley, Hoover's Secretary of War, had ordered General Douglas MacArthur, Army Chief of Staff, to execute the permanent removal of the

Bonus Army: "The President has just informed me that the civil government of the District of Columbia has reported to him that it is unable to maintain law and order in the District. You will have United States troops proceed immediately to the scene of disorder. Cooperate fully with the District of Columbia police force which is now in charge. Surround the affected area and clear it without delay. Turn over all prisoners to the civil authorities. In your orders insist that any women and children who may be in the affected area be accorded every consideration and kindness. Use all humanity consistent with the due execution of this order."

Douglas MacArthur

A portrait of Hurley

By the end of the day, the deed had been accomplished, but far from in any manner that might be considered considerate or kind. At 4:45 that afternoon, MacArthur led one infantry and one cavalry regiment against the mostly unarmed occupants. Assisting him was Major George Patton, who commanded six battle tanks that moved up Pennsylvania Avenue. Washington's Civil Service Workers, bored and tired of sweltering in stuffy offices, heard the commotion and turned out to see what all the excitement was about.

Patton

At first, the confused veterans and their families thought they had finally won their battle and that the marchers they were seeing, the ones who wore the same uniforms they had in worn in their youth, were marching in their honor. Then, their pride turned to terror when Patton ordered his men to charge the helpless citizens. The armed soldiers, with their bayonets fixed, quickly made their way through the crowd, driving men, women and children out of their most recent homes ahead of them. An anonymous observer later claimed, "Across the bridge the troops are coming. Police clear the road for them. An excited mass of citizens is pushed to the eastside of the bridge. They obey without protest. A better ordered crowd never gathered to witness a battle. But their sympathies, it is evident, were with the men in the darkness below. Along came the infantry, glistening bayonets fixed to their rifles. From the crowded spectators a chorus of boos is heard. The infantrymen threw gas grenades recklessly into the crowd of citizens. Fumes get into the eyes of the women and children. There is a scramble to escape from gas. The Army men go down into the open field. A truck of the district fire department goes behind them, throwing the floodlights as far as the first row of tents and hovels. The families are fast preparing to be evicted. The infantry advances cautiously. There is a line of shacks which had been erected for veterans with families. They were deserted, the women and children screaming away. The soldiers apply the torch. Then come the cavalry. The soldiers personally seemed to have little relish for the job ahead of them. Representatives of the veterans came out of the darkness to meet the soldiers, to tell them their women and children needed a little more time. Many of their 'things' were destroyed by fire. Men lined up in the shanty streets with packs strapped to their backs. Some of these were moving out of the Camp. Others are standing fast, perhaps still undecided. There are stragglers everywhere. They are hunting for lost buddies in the darkness."

Pictures of Army soldiers with gas masks confronting Bonus Army members

Of all the terrible things that happened that day, perhaps none was as ignoble or treacherous as the way in which innocent women and children were treated. The witness asserted, "Back on the hillside in the dark is a huddle of women. They had no word out of the darkness. They are awaiting the sound of shots which they fear may come as they did at the Pennsylvania Avenue eviction. A tower of flame burst from the camp. The big gospel tent is on fire, then the Salvation Army tent. The fire spreads as tents, sheds, cabins, coops, dog holes, beds, old autos, bureaus, boxes, wood, chairs, benches, food and everything else they had were consumed. Clouds of smoke arise above the flames. Tear gas is thrown into all the huts to drive the victims out before the torch was applied. Hundreds of these poor people suffered from the shock, and from wounds and accidents which the fright, confusion and fire created. Swords and bayonets were used to brad on more hurriedly the exhausted victims trudging toward the dark country with their packs. The soldiers and cavalry pursued these thousands of ex-service men and their families slowly and persistently into dark country roads, and then on those roads for miles until they had gotten beyond the district line (5 miles). Some of them escaped to Camp Bartlett, two miles back on a hill, and, knowing that it was a hospitable private camp, lodged there for the night. Others fell into the ditches, or strolled off into road-side woods. But by two o'clock in the morning Camp Marks was cleared of occupants and the huts and tents were in ashes. They were still smoking when I saw them after daylight."

A Bonus Army camp on fire

Much later that evening, while most of the city slept, Hurley called a press conference so that he and MacArthur might field any questions from reporters who would be trying to get in their articles for the next day. For his part, MacArthur claimed, "At that time I sent word by General [Pelham D.] Glassford to the various camps that I was going to evacuate them, clear Government property and that I hoped that they would not be humiliated by being forced out. I hoped that they would take advantage of the time element and evacuate without trouble. We moved down

Pennsylvania to the avenue area. … That mob down there was a bad looking mob. It was animated by the essence of revolution. The gentleness, the consideration, with which they had been treated had been mistaken for weakness and they had come to the conclusion, beyond the shadow of a doubt, that they were about to take over in some arbitrary way either the direct control of the Government or else to control it by indirect methods. It is my opinion that had the President not acted today, had he permitted this thing to go on for 24 hours more, he would have been faced with a grave situation which would have caused a real battle. Had he let it go on another week, I believe that the institutions of our Government would have been very severely threatened. I think it can be safely said that he had not only reached the end of an extraordinary patience but that he had gone to the very limit in his desire to avoid friction and trouble before he used force. Had he not used it at that time, I believe he would have been very derelict indeed in the judgment in which he was handling the safety of the country. This was the focus of the world today, and had he not acted with the force and vigor that he did, it would have been a very sad day for the country tomorrow."

MacArthur also insisted that it was not his soldiers but the inhabitants themselves who set the fires, but this seemed highly unlikely. If the soldiers did not set the fires, then it is likely that they spread by accident as unattended cooking fires warming the evening meals were kicked over and allowed to spread. Regardless, MacArthur alleged, "All done by the bonus marchers themselves; all done by the elements that were causing the trouble. I call them 'insurrectionists.' There were, in my opinion, few veteran soldiers in the group that we cleared out today--few indeed. … The Anacostia Camp was large. It took more time to evacuate it. I didn't want to cause physical harm and wanted to avoid as far as I could any hardship. I halted my own command and waited till about 9:00 until moving on Anacostia. All of these moves, of course, had been at the solicitation of the District Commissioners, the District Government. They requested not only that those areas should be evacuated by the military but they requested through General Glassford, speaking for Commissioner [Luther H.] Reichelderfer and Commissioner [Herbert B.] Crosby, that we proceed from Anacostia and evacuate the areas at Camp Meigs, at Camp Simms, and at a locality near the 7th Street docks and another locality that was near the Library in the 200 block on A Street. When we reached Anacostia the camp was practically abandoned. The control line of shacks were fired. There were a few people in the interior of the camp still packing and they were given full opportunity and time to go. They must have fired it themselves. It was burning when we got there. There were just the frontline shacks. I think had we been an hour later the whole camp would have been burned. Those people at that camp evacuated when I arrived. They were apparently bound for Camp Bartlett. The movement ceased at Anacostia."

To add insult to injury, and in an attempt to bolster his always sensitive ego, MacArthur went on to paint himself in the role of great liberator: "I have never seen greater relief on the part of the distressed populace than I saw today. I have released in my day more than one community which had been held in the grip of a foreign enemy. I have gone into villages that for 3 1/2 years had been under the domination of the soldiers of a foreign nation. I know what gratitude means along that line. I have never seen, even in those days, such expressions of gratitude as I heard from the crowds today. At least a dozen people told me, especially in the Negro section, that a regular system of tribute was being levied on them by this insurrectionist group; a reign of terror was being started which may have led to a system of Caponeism, and I believe later to insurgency and insurrection."

The problem was that MacArthur inflicted most of the harm on the residents by his own volition, after Hoover, his legitimate Commander-in-Chief, ordered him to stop the assault on the civilians. While no one was killed directly because of the attacks, one pregnant woman suffered a miscarriage and an infant died, at least in part due to exposure to tear gas. Another 55 people were injured.

Chapter 6: The Reverse Principle

"The then Governor Roosevelt of New York, a candidate for the Presidency, was quick to see, what his considerate nature would surely have made him feel, namely, that such a principle of government could not be made to go down in a democracy of intelligent human beings. Therefore, he inaugurated as a conspicuous part of his promised New Deal the reverse principle, namely, that of giving Federal-aid-to-the-poor. … All Roosevelt Republicans date back to the economic policy which came to a test in the Bonus March and the Evacuation. Now, since the Federal policy of 'no aid' invoked against the 10,000 poor World War veterans, when they hiked to Washington for relief in their distress, brought about the defeat of the Republican Party and was the forerunner of the New Deal, it is a matter of greatly renewed interest to have formally recorded the story of that expedition; how the men were received and treated, on what facts the Administration then acted, and whether its surface reason (riots) for exiling them from the City was true or a political alibi. I therefore see a new demand for publishing the historical facts, because there has been, and, I assume, always will be, a political party tendency to color or suppress the true facts in order to palliate President Hoover's conduct at that time. The facts did not justify President Hoover's order of evacuation." – John Henry Bartlett, *The Bonus March and the New Deal* (1937)

The following morning, on July 29, Hoover wrote to the Commissioners of the District of Columbia about the incident the day before: "In response to your information that the police of the District were overwhelmed by an organized attack by several thousand men, and were unable to maintain law and order, I complied with your request for aid from the Army to the police. It is a matter of satisfaction that, after the arrival of this assistance, the mobs which were defying the municipal government were dissolved without the firing of a shot or the loss of a life. I wish to call attention of the District Commissioners to the fact that martial law has not been declared; that responsibility for order still rests upon your commission and the police. The civil government of Washington must function uninterrupted. The Commissioners, through their own powers, should now deal with this question decisively. It is the duty of the authorities of the District to at once find the instigators of this attack on the police and bring them to justice. It is obvious that, after the departure of the majority of the veterans, subversive influences obtained control of the men remaining in the District, a large part of whom were not veterans, secured repudiation of their elected leaders and inaugurated and organized this attack. They were undoubtedly led to believe that the civil authorities could be intimidated with impunity because of attempts to conciliate by lax enforcement of city ordinances and laws in many directions. I shall expect the police to strictly enforce every ordinance of the District in every part of the city. I wish every violator of the law to be instantly arrested and prosecuted under due process of law."

While the commissioners might have been easy to convince, the American people were a different matter. Many had fathers, husbands or sons who had fought in the war, and they believed firmly in the veterans' cause. Others without a military background were also suffering similar fates as those who had been run off and understandably sympathized with their plights. Hoover, facing a swiftly approaching reelection bid, tried to convince them that he had done the right thing in his statement on July 29: "A challenge to the authority of the United States Government has been met, swiftly and firmly. After months of patient indulgence, the Government met overt lawlessness as it always must be met if the cherished processes of self-government are to be preserved. We cannot tolerate the abuse of constitutional rights by those who would destroy all government, no matter who they may be. Government cannot be coerced by mob rule. The Department of Justice is pressing its investigation into the violence which forced the call for Army detachments, and it is my sincere hope that those agitators who inspired yesterday's attack upon the Federal authority may be brought speedily to trial in the civil courts. There can be no safe harbor in the United States of America for violence. Order and civil tranquility are the first requisites in the great task of economic reconstruction to which our whole people now are devoting their heroic and noble energies. This national effort must not be retarded in even the slightest degree by organized lawlessness. The first obligation of my office is to uphold and defend the Constitution and the authority of the law. This I propose always to do."

Attempting to bolster the legitimacy of his decision, Hoover also released a copy of a charge given by Judge Oscar Luhring to a grand jury for the District of Columbia. In his instructions, Luhring told jurors, "The Court must take notice of the startling news appearing in the public press yesterday afternoon and this morning. It appears that a considerable group of men, styling themselves as bonus marchers, have come to the District of Columbia from all parts of the country for the stated purpose of petitioning Congress for the passage of legislation providing for the .immediate payment of the so-called bonus certificates. The number of these men has been variously estimated as from five to ten thousand. It is reported that certain buildings in this city, belonging to the Government, were in the possession of members of this so-called bonus army, who had been requested to vacate but had declined to do so; that possession of the property by the Government was immediately necessary for the erection of new buildings which Congress had directed built; that yesterday agents of the Treasury, proceeding lawfully, went upon the premises to dispossess the bonus army, and a force of district police was present to afford protection and prevent disorder; that the bonus marchers were removed from one old building which the public contractor was waiting to demolish; that thereupon a mob of several thousand bonus marchers, coming from other quarters, proceeded to this place for the purpose of resisting the officials and of regaining possession of the Government property."

Luhring

Luhring went on to support the government's position that it had only taken actions necessary to serve the people of the United States: "It appears that this mob, incited by some of their number, attacked the police, seriously injured a number of them, and engaged in riot and disorder. Their acts of resistance reached such a point that the police authorities were unable to maintain order and the Commissioners of the District were compelled to call upon the Federal authorities for troops to restore order and protect life and property. It is obvious that the laws of the District were violated in many respects. You should undertake an immediate investigation of these events with a view to bringing to justice those responsible for this violence, and those inciting it as well as those who took part in acts of violence. It is reported that the mob guilty of actual violence included few men, and was made up mainly of communists, and other disorderly elements. I hope you will find that is so and that few men who have worn the Nation's uniform engaged in this violent attack upon law and order. In the confusion not many arrests have been made, and it is said that many of the most violent disturbers and criminal elements in the unlawful gathering have already scattered and escaped from the city, but it may be possible yet to identify and apprehend them and bring them to justice."

However, in spite of his best efforts, there was little Hoover could do to save his reputation or his presidency. The country was angry at him and with how the veterans had been treated. On August 8, *Time* magazine ran an article describing the victims: "When war came in 1917 William Hushka, 22-year-old Lithuanian, sold his St. Louis butcher shop, gave the proceeds to his wife, joined the Army. He was sent to Camp Funston, Kansas where he was naturalized. Honorably discharged in 1919, he drifted to Chicago, worked as a butcher, seemed unable to hold a steady job. His wife divorced him, kept his small daughter. Long jobless, in June he joined a band of veterans marching to Washington to fuse with the Bonus Expeditionary Force. 'I might as well starve there as here', he told his brother. He took part in the demonstration at the Capital the day Congress adjourned without voting immediate cashing of the bonus. Last week William Hushka's Bonus for $528 suddenly became payable in full when a police bullet drilled him dead in the worst public disorder the capital has known in years."

Bartlett also saw the two men killed as martyrs of sorts: "Yesterday, Sunday, the seventh day of August, 1932, some haunting emotion urged me to motor over to Arlington Cemetery, just to observe where were buried WILLIAM J. HUSHKA and ERIC CARLSON, veterans killed by poverty. ... 'Buddie Bill,' as they called poor Hushka, was shot through the heart when unarmed and defenseless, standing aside with his coat over his arm, prepared to abandon the miserable hovel which he had come to look upon as the only home he had on earth. Yes, he had dwelt on Government owned land, a hungry, ragged, and disheartened veteran of the World War, a man of 35, of clean boyish countenance, of decent life, of consistent loyalty, a survivor of daring war service in France. He had committed no crime, save being poor. ...he and Buddy Carlson had trekked from among Oakland's unemployed sufferers to the home city of their Fatherland.... Yet even so, they were turning peacefully before the saber, when into their defenseless bodies chugged the lead, which, let it be said, conveyed to each a legal right to remain on or in a small lot of federal soil, as heroes, in perpetuity. The death-dealing missiles also bequeathed to their legal representatives the right by law to receive the bonus money, at once, which would have saved their lives had it been paid before. Yes, you, Hushka, and you, Carlson, are the only world war veterans who won the things for which you came."

In the end, few were surprised or disappointed when Hoover was defeated by Franklin Delano Roosevelt in the presidential election in November 1932. In fact, some felt that the Bonus Army, and the way it had been treated, led at least in part to Hoover's downfall.

Roosevelt

Given that they helped him win the White House, one might think that Roosevelt would have supported the veterans' claims for their bonuses. However, he opposed such legislation, ironically agreeing with Hoover that it would place too much burden on federal coffers. Still, Roosevelt had as much talent at making himself popular as Hoover did in making himself despised, and when another group of veterans marched on Washington in May 1933, he provided them with safe and clean campgrounds in nearby Virginia and even sent his own wife, the popular Eleanor, to visit them. Later, he changed the rules of the Civilian Conservation Corps to allow 25,000 veterans to join, enabling them to earn the living they needed to at least help support their families.

In the end, when Congress finally passed the Adjusted Compensation Payment Act in 1936, it had to override Roosevelt's veto in order to dispense $2 million in World War I bonuses. The men and their families finally had the thing they had fought so long for: enough money to make a fresh start, or to survive the situation they found themselves in.

What few could have known, however, was that in just a few years these same men, or their sons, would be called on to fight again. This time around, things would be different, and no group of fighting men in American history would ever be as well cared for as the "Greatest Generation" that won World War II.

Online Resources

<u>Other books about 20th century American history</u> by Charles River Editors

<u>Other books about the Bonus Army</u> on Amazon

Bibliography

Bartlett, John H. (1937)The Bonus March and the New Deal, Chicago: M. A. Donohue & Company

Daniels, Roger. (1971). The Bonus March: An Episode of the Great Depression. Westport, CT: Greenwood Publishing.

Dickson, Paul, and Thomas B. Allen. (2004). The Bonus Army: An American Epic. New York: Walker and Company.

Lisio, Donald J. (1974). The President and Protest: Hoover, Conspiracy, and the Bonus Riot. Columbia, MO: University of Missouri Press.

Made in United States
North Haven, CT
12 April 2024